Preface

Marketing is an essential aspect of any organization, and churches are no exception. In today's digital age, it's more important than ever for churches to have a strong online presence and effective marketing strategies in order to connect with their communities and attract new members. **This book includes various strategies that can help you build a thriving community and following, which is crucial for balancing member retention with other goals during the significant global challenge we face.**

As a result, we have compiled this book on Church Marketing, with the goal of providing practical advice and insights on how to create a successful church marketing strategy. This book is designed for church leaders, volunteers, and staff members who are looking to improve their marketing efforts and reach their goals.

Throughout this book, we cover a range of topics, from understanding your target audience and creating engaging content, to utilizing social media and measuring success. We draw on the expertise of marketing professionals, church leaders, and other experts to provide a comprehensive guide that can be tailored to your church's unique needs and goals.

We believe that marketing is an important tool for churches to reach and serve their communities, and we hope that this book will inspire you to take action and make a positive impact in the world. Whether you're just getting started with marketing or looking to take your strategy to the next level, we believe that the insights and tips in this book will help you achieve success. Thank you for joining us on this journey, and we wish you all the best in your marketing endeavors.

Sincerely,

Rev. Anthony R Caraway

In the modern age of technology and social media, marketing has become an essential component of every business and organization, including churches. Churches often struggle with attracting and retaining members, especially the younger generation, and effective marketing can help address these challenges. This ebook aims to provide churches with practical tips and strategies for successful marketing. Before we get into the depths of marketing let's think about three things: The Approach , Being On One Accord, and Willing Workers. I hope that you will take some of these topics and discuss with your colleagues, meditate, and pray.

The Approach:

Your approach to marketing is highly important even if it's passive, aggressive, or strategically falling in between. However, many marketers want you to consider utilizing the 80/20 rule. The 80/20 rule, also known as the Pareto Principle, is a concept that suggests that 80% of your results come from 20% of your efforts given to social media use. This means that 80% of your engagement, reach, and interactions with your audience come from 20% of your social media content. This means that you should aim to focus on creating high-quality, engaging content that resonates with your audience, rather than simply churning out a large volume of content. It's important to focus on the 20% of content that drives the most engagement. You can maximize your social media impact and build a loyal following.

Pareto Principle

80%

of time should be spent on where you want results

In practice, this may mean spending more time crafting thoughtful and compelling posts, sharing user-generated content, and engaging with your followers through comments, direct messages, and other interactions. It also means tracking and analyzing your social media metrics to identify which content is performing best and adjusting your strategy accordingly. The 80/20 rule is not a hard and fast rule, but it can be a useful guideline for prioritizing your social media efforts. You must maximize your impact on the platforms that matter most to your audience. Another layer to the 80/20 rule is choosing the platforms that you want to engage on. Let's say you are on 4 platforms: Youtube, Facebook, Instagram, and Twitter. The key is choosing how you want to engage on each platform. However, don't neglect making a solid decision on which platform you will spend most of your time as well as master engaging on that platform. This means you will spend 80% of your time on that platform and your followers will know you most from this. The remaining platforms will receive minor activity that will prayerfully draw them to the main source The goal is to draw people to, website, the priority media before mentioned, your church, and ultimately closer to God.

On One Accord

In today's fast-paced and ever-changing business world, organizations must develop a strong brand identity and effective marketing strategy to stand out from the competition. However, achieving this requires a unified and consistent approach to branding, communication, and marketing across all departments and stakeholders. The concept of being "on one accord" within an organization is essential for the development of a successful branding, communication, and marketing strategy. In other words, it takes more than just the marketing manager, more than just one person posting on social media, but there has to be a valiant effort by the leaders, workers, and church members to engage and share content.

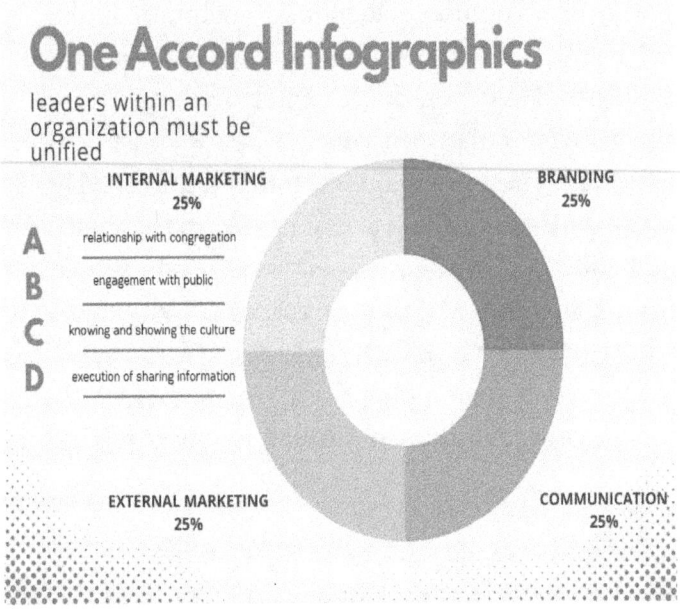

One Accord Infographics

leaders within an
organization must be
unified

INTERNAL MARKETING
25%

BRANDING
25%

A   relationship with congregation

B   engagement with public

C   knowing and showing the culture

D   execution of sharing information

EXTERNAL MARKETING
25%

COMMUNICATION
25%

Your organization must have a unified approach to branding, communication, and marketing. Branding is the process of creating a unique identity for your business, product or service in the minds of your target audience. It encompasses all the ways in which a company presents itself to the public, including its name, logo, design, messaging, and values. The main goal of branding is to establish a strong and memorable presence in the market, and to differentiate your business from competitors. Branding aims to create an emotional connection with your audience that goes beyond just your products or services.

Marketing, on the other hand, is the process of promoting your products or services to potential customers. It includes a variety of tactics such as advertising, public relations, sales promotions, events, and content marketing. The main goal of marketing is to generate interest, leads, and sales. Marketing focuses on identifying and understanding the needs and wants of your target audience, and then creating and delivering messages that speak directly to those needs.

In summary, branding is about creating a unique identity and emotional connection with your audience, while marketing is about promoting and selling your products or services to that audience. Effective branding can help support and strengthen your marketing efforts, as a strong brand can make your marketing messages more memorable and impactful.

Organizations can achieve a range of benefits, including improved engagement, increased brand loyalty, and more effective use of resources. By working together, departments can ensure that their efforts are aligned and consistent, resulting in a more effective overall strategy.

The brand identity of an organization is the foundation of its marketing strategy, and a consistent approach to branding can help organizations create a strong brand identity that resonates. When you are marketing it is only an extension or advertisement of how you function. Yes, you can make yourself look better online than you really are, but I have witnessed it backfire. The key elements of a brand identity, such as logo, messaging, and visual identity, should be implemented across all communication channels to ensure consistency and reinforce the brand image. Be authentically great at who you are. Sometimes this may require rebranding what already exists.

In conclusion, being on one accord within an organization is crucial for developing a strong, cohesive brand identity and effective marketing strategy. By taking a unified approach to branding, communication, and marketing, organizations can achieve a range of benefits and stand out from the competition. With the strategies outlined in this book, organizations can create a culture of consistency and collaboration, leading to greater success and growth.

Willing Workers

Exodus 18:21-23 teaches us about the value of willing workers in any organization. In this passage, Moses' father-in-law Jethro advises him to appoint capable men to serve as leaders and judges for the people. Jethro suggests that these leaders should be individuals who fear God, are trustworthy, and hate dishonest gain.

Above all, Jethro emphasizes the importance of finding men who are willing to serve: 'But select capable men from all the people—men who fear God, trustworthy men who hate dishonest gain—and appoint them as officials over thousands, hundreds, fifties and tens. Have them serve as judges for the people at all times, but have them bring every difficult case to you; the simple cases they can decide themselves. That will make your load lighter, because they will share it with you. If you do this and God commands, you will be able to stand the strain, and all these people will go home satisfied.'

The excerpt emphasizes the significance of leaders who possess the requisite skills and qualities and are eager to serve, as they play a crucial role in the success of any organization. In the absence of dedicated and committed workers, a leader's responsibilities can become too burdensome, leading to subpar results. Therefore, it is vital to identify competent and enthusiastic individuals who can contribute to the organization's growth. This enables leaders to assign tasks and concentrate their efforts on critical matters, promoting the organization's overall prosperity.

The number of people needed on a church marketing team can vary depending on the size and needs of the church. Here are some factors to consider:

1. Church size: A larger church with more programs, events, and outreach initiatives may require a larger marketing team to manage all the marketing efforts.
2. Marketing goals: If the church has ambitious marketing goals, such as launching a new website, increasing attendance, or expanding outreach efforts, a larger team may be needed to execute these goals in a short period of time
3. Available resources: A smaller church with limited resources may need to rely on a smaller marketing team or even a single person to manage marketing efforts.
4. Skillset and expertise: It's important to have people on the marketing team with a variety of skills and expertise, such as graphic design, copywriting, social media management, and data analysis.

Finding marketing help inside the church can be a great way to tap into the talents and skills of your congregation members. Many churches have individuals with backgrounds in marketing, communications, graphic design, or social media who are eager to offer their services to their church community. Consider reaching out to your congregation through church announcements or newsletters to ask if anyone is interested in volunteering their marketing expertise. You may also consider creating a marketing committee within your church to oversee and implement marketing efforts. By tapping into the resources within your congregation, you can save on costs while also creating a sense of community involvement and ownership over your church's marketing initiatives.

Where's The Help?

There's a person in every department that can assist with marketing no matter their skill level or age.

When you look at this illustration you already have 8 people

In general, a small to medium-sized church may be able to manage their marketing efforts with a team of 2-3 people, while a larger church may need a team of 5-10 people. However, it's important to focus on quality over quantity, and to make sure the marketing team has the necessary skills and resources to achieve the church's marketing goals.

The modern era has introduced a new age of evangelism so it may be a good idea to train leaders and ministers who are not dedicated media team workers in basic operations in marketing. For instance, if I am ill and have to miss church, someone in the church knows how to turn on the computer, someone knows how to turn on the camera and someone knows how to press the record button. etc. We have to make sure in our marketing efforts and planning that churches are not suffering because individuals are absent or quit.

TABLE OF CONTENTS

Chapter 1: Defining Your Church's Unique Identity and Value

Before developing a marketing plan, it is essential to understand what sets your church apart from others. What is your unique value proposition? What makes your church special and different? This chapter will guide churches through a process of defining their unique value proposition, which will serve as the foundation for all marketing efforts.

Chapter 2: Building an Effective Website

A website is often the first point of contact for people looking for information about a church. A well-designed and informative website can help churches attract and retain visitors. This chapter will provide practical tips for building an effective church website, including design, content, and search engine optimization (SEO).

Chapter 3: Social Media Marketing

Social media platforms have become an essential marketing tool for businesses and organizations, including churches. This chapter will explore how churches can effectively use social media to engage with members, reach out to the community, and attract new visitors. Topics covered include content creation, social media platforms, and best practices for engagement.

Chapter 4: Email Marketing

Email marketing is a cost-effective and efficient way to communicate with members and potential visitors. This chapter will provide tips for building an email list, creating engaging email content, and measuring email marketing success.

Chapter 5: Advertising and Promotion

Advertising and promotion are critical components of any marketing plan. This chapter will explore various advertising and promotional strategies for churches, including online and offline methods. Topics covered include Google Ads, social media advertising, print materials, and events.

Chapter 6: Monitoring and Measuring Success

It is essential to monitor and measure the success of marketing efforts to understand what is working and what is not. This chapter will explore various tools and metrics for tracking marketing success, including website analytics, social media metrics, and email marketing metrics.

Chapter 7: Essential Marketing Equipment

In this chapter, we discuss the equipment and tools necessary for effective church marketing. The equipment you need for marketing will depend on the specific tactics and channels you plan to use.

Chapter 8: Growing Your Youtube Channel & Other Channels

In this chapter, you'll discover effective strategies for growing social media channels. Starting with the importance of creating engaging, informative, and relevant content to your audience. We'll also delve into driving traffic to your channel, build your brand presence, and expand your reach through advertising and influencer marketing. By the end of this chapter, you'll have the tools and knowledge to grow your social media presence, optimize your performance, and effectively reach new audiences.

Conclusion:

Marketing is vital for church growth and outreach. It involves defining a unique value proposition, building an effective website, using social media and email marketing, and implementing advertising and promotional strategies. By monitoring and measuring success, churches can refine their approach. Marketing creates a consistent brand message, attracting and retaining members. It targets specific demographics, using email marketing and social media advertising to reach interested individuals and increase engagement. By doing so, churches can grow and build a sense of community beyond Sunday services.

Chapter 1

Create a Unique Value Proposition

(Define and understand what sets a church apart from others)

A unique value proposition (UVP) is a statement that clearly and concisely communicates the unique benefit that a product, service, or organization provides to its customers or audience. It defines what sets the product, service, or organization apart from others in the marketplace and why someone should choose it over alternatives. A good UVP should be specific, clear, and memorable, and should address the needs, wants, or pain points of the target audience. To define and understand what sets your church apart from others, there are a few key steps you can take. First, identify your church's core values, which may include things like inclusivity, community, spirituality, or social justice. This will help you understand what your church stands for and what values are most important to your community. Next, understand and reflect on your church's mission statement, which should outline its purpose and objectives. This will communicate what your church hopes to accomplish and how it intends to do so.

Evaluating your church's strengths and weaknesses can also help you identify what your church does well and where it could improve. Consider the needs and concerns of your community to identify what your church can offer that is unique. For example, if your community lacks affordable childcare, your church may offer a low-cost or free daycare service. If you live in a food desert, your church may begin cultivating a garden. Analyzing your church's history can also offer insights into what sets it apart from others. Consider the historical events that have shaped your church and its community. These events may have led to unique traditions or perspectives that distinguish your church from others.Assessing your competition can also help you identify what makes your church unique in comparison. Take a look at other churches in your area and what they offer that your church does not.

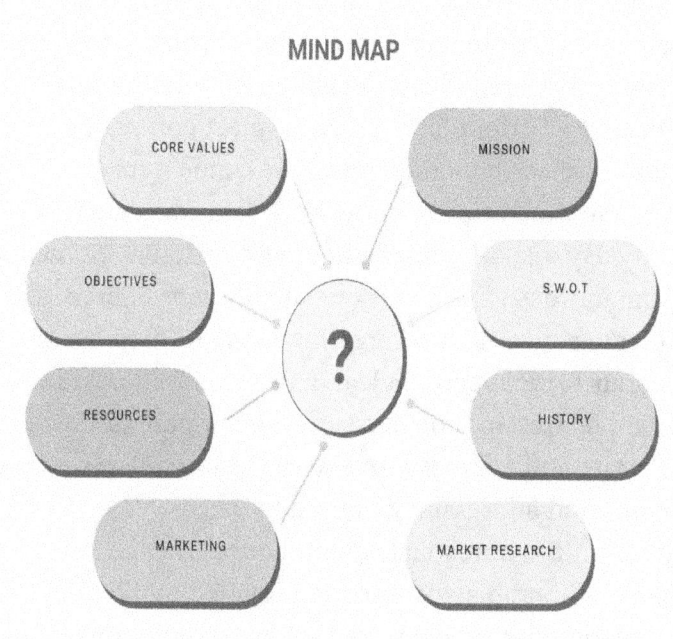

By taking these steps, you can define and understand what makes your church special and different. This knowledge will help you develop effective marketing strategies that communicate your unique value proposition and help you stand out in a crowded marketplace.

One effective way to organize and visualize these different components is to create a mind map. Start by placing the core values, objectives, resources, marketing, mission, SWOT analysis, church history, and market research in separate bubbles or nodes. From there, you can connect related ideas and concepts with lines or branches. For example, you can connect core values to mission to show how they relate, or connect market research to marketing to show how data can inform strategy. By visually organizing these different elements, you can more easily identify what sets your church apart and create a clear and compelling UVP. Remember to keep your UVP specific, clear, and memorable, and to focus on addressing the needs, wants, or pain points of your target audience. By leveraging your church's unique strengths and addressing community needs, you can create a UVP that resonates with your audience and helps your church stand out in a crowded marketplace. Mind mapping is a technique that helps to organize and visualize information in a way that can be easily understood and remembered. It involves creating a visual diagram that connects different ideas and concepts together, using images, colors, and symbols to represent them.

When applied to church marketing, mind mapping can be a powerful tool for creating a unique value proposition. By mapping out your church's core values, objectives, resources, marketing strategies, mission, SWOT analysis, church history, and market research, you can gain a better understanding of what sets your church apart from others in your community.

Through this process, you can identify the unique benefits and services that your church provides to its members and community. By creating a clear and concise UVP, you can communicate these benefits to potential members and stand out in a crowded marketplace of churches. In addition, mind mapping can help you identify areas for improvement and growth within your church. By analyzing your church's strengths and weaknesses, you can develop strategies to capitalize on your strengths and address your weaknesses.

Overall, mind mapping can be a valuable tool for developing a successful church marketing strategy. It can help you define your unique value proposition, understand your church's strengths and weaknesses, and develop effective marketing strategies to reach your target audience.

Chapter 2

Building An Effective Church Website

Including Design, Content, and Search Engine Optimization (SEO)

Building an effective church website requires careful consideration of design, content, and search engine optimization (SEO). Here are some practical tips to help you create a website that engages visitors and supports your ministry.

1. Design:

- Keep it clean and simple: Avoid clutter and choose a simple, easy-to-use design. Use plenty of white space to make the content stand out. Keep in mind that a range of audiences visit your site. So you want to make it easy for everyone to navigate. Yes, you may have a professional designer create it but I encourage you to keep this in mind as you are requesting their service. The less you have on your site also assists in loading times.
- Use high-quality images: Use high-quality photos and graphics that convey your church's

personality and values. Avoid stock images that look generic and impersonal.

- Make it mobile-friendly: Ensure that your website is mobile-friendly and looks great on different devices.
- Use clear calls-to-action: Make it easy for visitors to take action by including clear calls-to-action (CTAs) throughout your website.

2. **Content**:

- Use clear, concise language: Use simple, easy-to-understand language that communicates your message clearly.
- Highlight your mission and values: Make sure your website communicates your church's mission and values, and why they matter.
- Share your story: Share stories of how your church is making a difference in people's lives. This can help visitors connect with your ministry on a personal level.
- Use video: Use video to tell your church's story, share testimonials, and showcase your ministries.

3. **SEO**:

- Use relevant keywords: Use relevant keywords throughout your website to help search engines understand what your website is about. There are search engines specialized in generating keywords for websites, social media, and other relative marketing techniques.

- Optimize your content: Ensure that your website's content is optimized for search engines by including title tags, meta descriptions, and header tags.
- Build links: Build links from other websites to your website to help improve your website's search engine rankings.
- Use local SEO: Use local SEO techniques to help your website rank higher in local search results.

As you can see there are levels to your website and SEO. Many businesses make business plans before they move forward with this so that they may be able to fluidly execute their marketing efforts such as websites or social media. Within a Business plan is a Marketing plan. This is something you should consider before creating or revamping your current marketing plan. A marketing plan is where you ask yourself all of the important questions and do a comparative analysis to other businesses. People always run away from doing a business plan even in consultations. Then they will come back to me months later asking questions that could have been answered if they did a business plan or at least a feasibility statement in the beginning. Just because a church has been around for a long time doesn't mean it doesn't need to evaluate its business plan or feasibility from time to time. Churches, like any other organization, are subject to changes in the social, economic, and cultural landscape, and may need to adapt to meet the evolving needs of their congregation and community. A renewed business plan or feasibility statement can help churches identify areas for improvement and growth, and develop strategies to address them. It can also help them assess their financial sustainability and identify opportunities for fundraising or revenue generation. By taking the time to evaluate their current position and plan for the future, churches can ensure that they remain relevant and impactful in their communities for years to come. Here is an outline of a sample marketing plan:

Executive Summary

- Brief overview of the marketing plan
- Summary of the company's objectives, target market, and marketing goals

II. Situation Analysis

- Company analysis: mission, vision, values, and goals
- Market analysis: target market, trends, and competition

- SWOT analysis: strengths, weaknesses, opportunities, and threats

III. Marketing Objectives

- Specific, measurable, and achievable goals
- Aligned with the company's overall objectives
- Time-bound and relevant to the target market

IV. Marketing Strategies

- Product: positioning, features, benefits, and packaging
- Price: pricing strategy, discounts, and payment terms
- Promotion: advertising, sales promotions, personal selling, and public relations
- Place: channels of distribution, logistics, and inventory management

V. Implementation Plan

- Detailed action plan with timelines and responsibilities
- Budget allocation for each marketing mix element
- Metrics and monitoring plan to measure success

VI. Evaluation and Control

- Regular review of marketing plan against objectives
- Key performance indicators to measure success
- Contingency plan in case of unexpected events or changes in the market

VII. Conclusion

- Recap of the marketing plan and its importance to the company's success
- Call to action for implementation of the plan

The above are basic elements of a business plan that will help with moving your marketing forward. Here are some more advanced things to include in a business plan that will not only help with your marketing and planning but also help with attraction to donors and sponsors for projects your organization is interested in.

Components	Purpose or Definition	Examples
External Analysis	Understanding the external environment and competition	PESTEL analysis, SWOT analysis, Porter's Five Forces
Internal Analysis	Evaluating the internal environment and capabilities of the company	Value Chain Analysis, Resource-Based View, SWOT Analysis
Mission Statement	A statement that defines the company's purpose and objectives	"To provide affordable and high-quality healthcare services to underserved communities"
Vision Statement	A statement that describes the company's long-term aspirations	"To be the leading provider of sustainable energy solutions worldwide"
Value Proposition	A statement that communicates the unique benefit of the company's products or services	"The only diet plan designed specifically for new moms to help them lose weight and regain energy"

Marketing Mix	A set of tactical tools used to implement the marketing strategy	Product, Price, Place, Promotion
Sales Strategy	A plan to identify, target, and sell products or services to customers	Direct sales, online sales, telemarketing, retail sales
Financial Projections	Forecasting future financial performance based on current and historical data	Income statement, cash flow statement, balance sheet
Implementation Plan	A detailed plan outlining how the marketing strategy will be executed	Timelines, budgets, resource allocation
Evaluation and Control	A plan to monitor and measure the success of the marketing strategy	Key performance indicators, metrics, benchmarks

Chapter 3

Effective Practices of Social Media Engagement

Here are some examples of effective best practices for social media engagement:

1. Consistency: Consistently posting and engaging with followers is key. Create a content calendar to keep a consistent posting schedule and ensure that you're engaging with followers in a timely manner.
2. Authenticity: Be authentic and genuine in your social media interactions. Show your followers who you are and what your church stands for. Avoid using stock images and generic language.
3. Visual content: Use high-quality visual content to grab your followers' attention. Share images, videos, and graphics that convey your message and engage your audience.
4. Respond to comments: Respond to comments and messages from followers in a timely manner. This shows that you value their input and are actively engaged with your community.

5. Share user-generated content: Share user-generated content to encourage engagement and build a sense of community. This could include reposting photos or testimonials from followers.
6. Use hashtags: Use relevant hashtags to help your content get discovered by new followers. Use hashtags that are specific to your church or ministry, as well as more general hashtags that relate to your content.
7. Encourage engagement: Encourage your followers to engage with your content by asking questions, hosting polls, or inviting them to share their own experiences.
8. Monitor analytics: Monitor your social media analytics to see which types of content are resonating with your followers and adjust your strategy accordingly.

Content Creation

Here are some examples of effective social media engagement from churches:

1. Saddleback Church: Saddleback Church frequently shares user-generated content from their congregation, such as photos and

testimonials, to encourage engagement and build a sense of community.

2. Life.Church: Life.Church uses visually appealing graphics and videos to communicate their message and engage their audience.

3. Hillsong Church: Hillsong Church frequently shares behind-the-scenes photos and videos to give followers a glimpse into their church and ministry.

By following these best practices and learning from successful examples, you can effectively engage your social media audience and build a strong online community for your church. Here are some platforms that allow you to manage and create content:

1. Canva: Canva is a free graphic design platform that allows you to create stunning graphics, social media posts, presentations, and more. It offers a wide range of templates and design tools that are easy to use, even for beginners.

2. Grammarly: Grammarly is a free writing assistant that helps you write clear and mistake-free content. It checks your spelling and grammar, suggests better words and phrases, and even

provides writing tips to help you improve your skills.

3. Hootsuite: Hootsuite is a social media management tool that helps you schedule and publish content across multiple platforms. It also provides analytics and insights to help you track your social media performance.

4. Google Analytics: Google Analytics is a free web analytics tool that helps you track your website traffic, user behavior, and conversions. It provides valuable insights into your audience and can help you optimize your content for better results.

5. Unsplash: Unsplash is a free stock photo website that offers high-quality images that you can use in your content. It has a vast library of images that are free to use, even for commercial projects.

6. YouTube Creator Academy: The YouTube Creator Academy is a free resource that provides tutorials and courses on how to create and optimize content for YouTube. It covers topics such as video production, editing, and optimization.

7. HubSpot Blog Topic Generator: The HubSpot Blog Topic Generator is a free tool that helps you come up with new blog post ideas. Simply enter a few keywords related to your topic, and the tool will generate a list of blog post titles for you.

By using these resources, even beginners can create high-quality content that engages their audience and supports their goals. Social media is a great way for churches to engage with their members and build a sense of community. The next page will reveal some tips for using social media effectively:

How can a church effectively use social media to engage with members

1. Post regular updates: Regularly post updates on your church's social media channels to keep your members informed about upcoming events, services, and other news. This helps to build anticipation and excitement for events and services.

2. Share photos and videos: Share photos and videos of your church services and events on social media to give members who couldn't attend a sense of what they missed. This helps to build a sense of community and connection.

3. Use social media to promote discussion: Use social media to encourage members to engage with each other by sharing their thoughts and experiences. This can be done through posting

questions, hosting polls, or inviting members to share their own stories.

4. Respond to comments and messages: Respond to comments and messages from members in a timely manner. This shows that you value their input and are actively engaged with your community.

5. Use hashtags: Use relevant hashtags to help your content get discovered by new members. Use hashtags that are specific to your church or ministry, as well as more general hashtags that relate to your content.

6. Share member stories: Share stories of members who have been impacted by your church or ministry. This helps to build a sense of community and encourages others to share their own stories.

7. Use live streaming: Use live streaming on social media to give members who can't attend in person the opportunity to participate in services and events in real-time.

8. Use social media to provide resources: Use social media to share resources that can help members grow in their faith, such as daily devotionals or inspirational quotes.

By following these tips, churches can effectively use social media to engage with their members and build a strong sense of community. The idea is to bridge the gap between the church and the world sort of like you do when you have a new membership program. When funneling a new member into a church there are several steps to help new members feel welcome and included in the church community.

Step 1: Invitation - When someone visits the church for the first time, they would be personally invited to participate in the Newcomers' Welcome Program.

Step 2: Orientation - The new member would attend an orientation session that provides an overview of the church's history, beliefs, and values. They would also be given a tour of the church building and introduced to key staff members and volunteers.

Step 3: Small Groups - The new member would be encouraged to join a small group that matches their interests or life stage. This could be a Bible study group, a prayer group, or a social group. This would provide a more intimate and supportive community within the larger church.

Step 4: Service Opportunities - The new member would be given opportunities to serve the church and its community. This could be through volunteering at the church's food pantry, participating in a mission trip, or serving on a ministry team. This would help the new member feel a sense of purpose and belonging in the church.

Step 5: Membership - After participating in the Newcomers' Welcome Program and getting involved in the church, the new member would be invited to become an official member of the church. This would involve a membership class and a commitment to the church's mission and values.

Overall, this funneling process is designed to help new members feel welcomed, connected, and engaged in the church community. This is the perspective we should take when we are engaged in marketing internally and externally.

How can a church effectively use social media to attract new visitors

Social media can be a powerful tool for churches to attract new visitors. Here are some tips for using social media effectively for outreach:

1. Create a welcoming social media presence: Make sure your social media profiles are up-to-date and reflect the welcoming and inclusive culture of your church. Use engaging visuals, such as high-quality photos and videos, to showcase your church and its activities.
2. Use targeted advertising: Use social media advertising to target people in your community who are likely to be interested in your church. You can target based on location, interests, and other demographics.
3. Promote events: Use social media to promote events that may appeal to people who are not regular church-goers. For example, you could host a free community concert or a workshop on a popular topic.
4. Share inspiring content: Share inspiring and uplifting content that appeals to people's values and interests. This can include quotes, Bible verses, and stories of people who have been positively impacted by your church.
5. Offer online resources: Offer online resources such as sermons or podcasts that are easily accessible to new visitors. This allows them to get to know your church and your teachings before attending in person.
6. Encourage sharing: Encourage your members to share your church's social media content with their friends and family. This can help to spread the word about your church to a wider audience.

7. Use social media influencers: Consider partnering with social media influencers who have a large following in your community. They can help to promote your church to their followers and attract new visitors.

By using these strategies, churches can effectively use social media to attract new visitors and grow their community.

Chapter 4

Email Marketing

Email marketing began in the late 1970s, shortly after the first email was sent in 1971. The first email marketing campaign is generally attributed to Gary Thuerk, a marketing manager at Digital Equipment Corporation, who sent the first unsolicited mass email on May 3, 1978, to promote a new line of computers. Thuerk's email campaign generated significant sales and demonstrated the potential of email as a marketing tool.

However, it was not until the 1990s, with the widespread adoption of personal computers and the growth of the internet, that email marketing became more widely used. By the mid-1990s, email marketing had become an established practice among businesses, with companies using email to reach out to customers and prospects, promote products and services, and build relationships with their audiences.

Today, email marketing remains a popular and effective tool for businesses of all sizes, with many companies using email marketing platforms and automation tools to manage their campaigns and reach a wider audience. Email marketing is the practice of sending commercial messages to a group of people via email. Here are some tips for building an email list, creating engaging email content, and measuring email marketing success:

1. Building an email list: The first step in email marketing is to build an email list. This can be done by asking people to sign up on your website or in-person events. You can also offer incentives such as a free e-book or a discount on merchandise for signing up.
2. Creating engaging email content: The content of your email is crucial to its success. Make sure your email is visually appealing, easy to read, and provides value to the reader. Include calls-to-action that encourage the reader to take action, such as registering for an event or donating to a cause.
3. Personalize your emails: Personalizing your emails can increase open rates and engagement. Use the recipient's name in the subject line and throughout the email. Segment your email list based on interests or behaviors to send targeted messages.
4. Measure email marketing success: To measure the success of your email marketing campaigns, you can track metrics such as open rates, click-through rates, and conversion rates. Use this data to optimize your future email campaigns.
5. Automate your emails: You can automate your email marketing campaigns using email marketing software. This allows you to send

personalized emails triggered by specific actions, such as when someone signs up for your email list or abandons their shopping cart.

6. Comply with email regulations: Make sure you comply with email regulations such as the CAN-SPAM Act by including an unsubscribe link in your emails and honoring unsubscribe requests promptly.

7. Test and optimize: Continuously test and optimize your email campaigns to improve their effectiveness. Experiment with different subject lines, calls-to-action, and visuals to see what works best for your audience.

By following these tips, churches can effectively use email marketing to build a community and engage with their members.

Chapter 5

Exploring Advertising and Marketing

Are you looking for effective ways to promote your church's events and services to a wider audience? Look no further than advertising and marketing strategies! By combining both online and offline methods, churches can reach a variety of demographics and engage with their congregation in meaningful ways. Online advertising platforms such as Google Ads and social media advertising can help target specific interests and behaviors, while print materials and events can generate buzz in the local community. Word of mouth is a powerful tool, and email marketing can provide targeted messaging to your church's email list. Additionally, optimizing your website for search engines can help potential new members find your church online. By utilizing these different strategies, churches can create a comprehensive marketing plan to reach their target audience and promote their events and services to the wider community. Here are some advertising and promotional strategies for churches, both online and offline:

1. Google Ads: Google Ads is an online advertising platform that allows you to create ads that appear in Google search results. Churches can use Google Ads to promote events, services, or their website. You can target specific keywords related to your church or location, and set a budget for your ad campaign.

2. Social media advertising: Social media platforms such as Facebook, Instagram, and Twitter offer advertising options that allow you to target specific demographics, interests, and behaviors. You can create ads that promote your church's events, services, or online content.

3. Print materials: Print materials such as flyers, brochures, and posters can be effective for promoting your church to people in your local community. You can distribute these materials at events or public places where people gather. Billboards may cost a great deal. However, they attract hundreds of thousands of onlookers per week or month

4. Events: Hosting events such as concerts, workshops, or community service activities can be a great way to promote your church to the wider community. You can use online and offline advertising methods to promote the event and encourage attendance.

5. Word of mouth: Word of mouth can be a powerful advertising tool for churches. Encourage your members to invite their friends and family to church services and events. Provide them with resources such as invitations or social media graphics to make it easy for them to spread the word.

6. Email marketing: As discussed earlier, email marketing can be an effective way to promote your church's events and services to your email list. You can segment your email list based on interests or behaviors to send targeted messages.

7. Search engine optimization (SEO): Optimizing your church's website for search engines can help people find your church online. Use relevant keywords on your website and create high-quality content that is shareable and engaging.

By using a combination of online and offline advertising and promotional strategies, churches can effectively promote their services, events, and online content to the wider community.

Chapter 6

The Metrics

In today's digital age, churches can no longer rely solely on traditional marketing methods to engage their congregation and reach new audiences. With the help of website analytics, social media metrics, email marketing metrics, conversion tracking, and A/B testing, churches can gain valuable insights into how their marketing efforts are performing and optimize their campaigns for better engagement and conversion. By tracking metrics such as website traffic, pageviews, reach, open rates, and conversion rates, churches can understand what types of content and messaging resonate with their audience and make data-driven decisions to improve their marketing strategies. In this way, churches can leverage the power of digital marketing to effectively engage their congregation and reach new audiences.

1. Website analytics: Website analytics tools like Google Analytics can provide insights into how people are finding and using your church's website. You can track metrics such as website traffic, pageviews, bounce rate, and time on site.

This data can help you optimize your website for better user experience and engagement.

2. Social media metrics: Social media platforms like Facebook, Instagram, and Twitter offer metrics that allow you to track the performance of your posts and ads. You can track metrics such as reach, engagement, clicks, and conversions. This data can help you understand what types of content and messaging resonate with your audience.

3. Email marketing metrics: Email marketing platforms like Mailchimp or Constant Contact offer metrics that allow you to track the performance of your email campaigns. You can track metrics such as open rates, click-through rates, and conversion rates. This data can help you optimize your email campaigns for better engagement and conversion.

4. Conversion tracking: Conversion tracking is the process of tracking when a website visitor completes a desired action, such as filling out a form or making a donation. You can use conversion tracking tools like Google Tag Manager or Facebook Pixel to track these actions and attribute them to specific marketing campaigns.

5. A/B testing: A/B testing is the process of testing two versions of a marketing campaign to see

which one performs better. You can use A/B testing tools like Optimizely or Google Optimize to test different versions of your website, social media posts, or email campaigns.

By using these tools and metrics, churches can track their marketing success and optimize their campaigns for better engagement and conversion. It's important to set clear goals and KPIs for each marketing campaign, and to regularly review and analyze the data to make informed decisions.

Chapter 7

Essential Marketing Equipment

While there are many tools and strategies for church marketing, word of mouth is still one of the most powerful tools at your disposal. However, if you're looking to expand your reach and create a more comprehensive marketing plan, you'll need to invest in some equipment and tools. The equipment you need for marketing will depend on the specific marketing tactics and channels you plan to use. A camera, computer, printer, and software are all essential for creating and managing marketing materials. If you plan to create video or audio content, you'll also need audio and video equipment. By prioritizing essential marketing equipment and tools, you can create a successful church marketing strategy that helps you reach and engage with your target audience. The equipment you need for marketing will depend on the specific marketing tactics and channels you plan to use. Here are some equipment options to consider:

1. Camera: A camera can be useful for taking photos and videos to use on your website, social media channels, and other marketing materials. Depending on your budget and needs, you may

want to consider a DSLR camera or a high-quality smartphone camera.

2. Computer: A computer is essential for creating and editing graphics, writing copy, managing social media channels, and other marketing tasks. Depending on your needs, you may want to consider a desktop computer or a laptop.

3. Software: There are a variety of software programs and tools that can be useful for marketing, such as Adobe Creative Suite for graphic design, Hootsuite for social media management, and Google Analytics for website analytics. Depending on your needs, you may want to invest in these tools to streamline your marketing efforts.

4. Printer: Many churches have printers today. However, there may be a need to upgrade what you have depending on your marketing plan. A printer can be useful for printing flyers, brochures, and other marketing materials. Depending on your needs, you may want to consider a high-quality inkjet or laser printer. If you can minimize your expenses on the church printer, you will be able to reduce the amount of money spent on companies that offer printing services for your convenience.

5. Audio and video equipment: In case you intend to create videos or podcasts for your marketing

campaign, it is advisable to think about purchasing audio and video equipment such as lighting, a microphone, and editing software. While having the ability to generate videos and audio content is great, the quality of the sound is crucial. Often, individuals do not realize this until they hear their voice or the sound quality during a live broadcast or presentation.

Effective marketing requires continuous effort and adaptability, so it's important to plan for future changes and allocate resources accordingly. Prioritize essential marketing equipment and tools based on your goals and channels. Advanced goals require an advanced team with a perpetual education plan. This book empowers you with the knowledge and tools to create a successful church marketing strategy, from understanding your target audience to measuring success. Experiment with various channels to find what works best for your church. With the right mindset and approach, your church can make a positive impact in your community. Thank you for joining me on this journey and best of luck in your marketing endeavors!

Chapter 8

Growing Your Channels

In this chapter, we'll explore effective strategies for growing your YouTube channel and other social media channels. We'll start by discussing the importance of creating high-quality content that is engaging, informative, and relevant to your audience.

Next, we'll dive into some key tactics for increasing your reach and engagement on YouTube, such as optimizing your video titles, descriptions, and tags, promoting your channel on social media, collaborating with other creators, and engaging with your audience through comments and community posts.

We'll also cover strategies for leveraging other social media platforms, such as Facebook, Instagram, Twitter, and LinkedIn, to drive traffic to your YouTube channel and grow your overall online presence. This includes creating shareable content, building a strong brand presence, and using paid advertising and influencer marketing to reach new audiences.

Finally, we'll discuss ways to measure and analyze your channel's performance, including tracking metrics such as views, watch time, and engagement, and using data to inform your content and marketing strategies. By the end of this chapter, you'll have a clear understanding of how to effectively grow your YouTube channel and other social media channels, and how to measure and optimize your success over time.

It's important to remember that the algorithm for social media channels is always changing. Platforms like Facebook, Instagram, TikTok, and Twitter are constantly updating their algorithms to provide the best user experience and to keep up with changing trends and user behaviors. This means that what worked in the past may not work in the future, and it's important to stay up-to-date on the latest algorithm changes and trends in order to effectively grow your following and engagement on these platforms. By staying informed and adapting your strategies accordingly, you can better navigate the ever-changing landscape of social media and stay ahead of the competition.

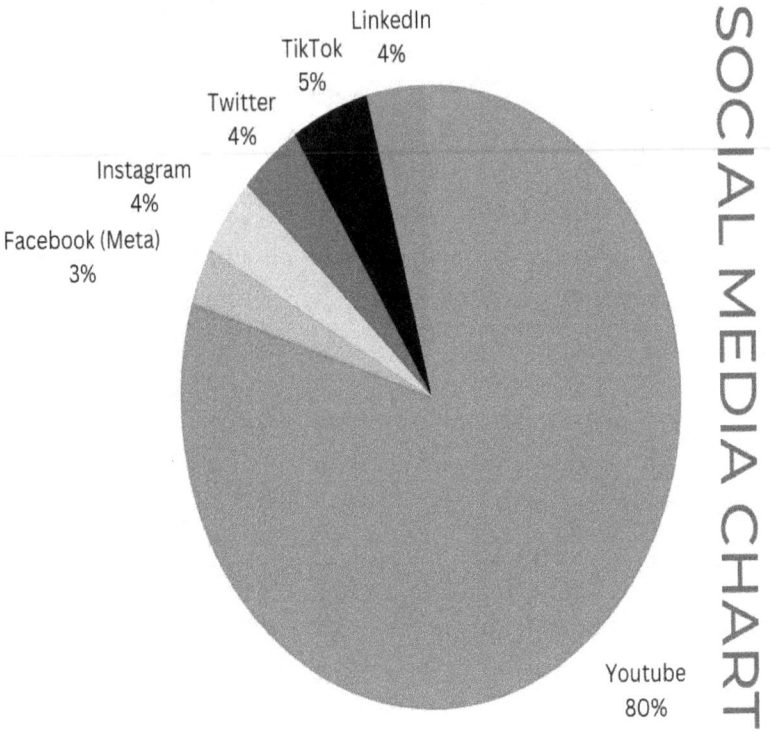

SOCIAL MEDIA CHART

Here are some tips to optimize your church YouTube channel's description to increase views, likes, and shares:

1. Make the description clear and concise: Ensure that your description is brief and clearly explains what your channel is about. Use keywords that

accurately describe your content to help people find your channel through search.

2. Include a call-to-action: Encourage viewers to like, share, and subscribe to your channel by including a call-to-action in your description. For example, you could say something like, "Don't forget to like, share, and subscribe to stay updated on our latest videos."

3. Highlight your unique selling point: Let viewers know what sets your channel apart from others by highlighting your unique selling point. This could be the quality of your videos, the frequency of your uploads, or the range of topics you cover.

4. Add links to your social media: Add links to your church's social media accounts to your description to help viewers connect with your community outside of YouTube. This will also help promote your channel to a wider audience.

5. Use relevant tags: Use relevant tags to help your videos appear in search results. This will make it easier for viewers to find your videos when searching for topics related to your content.

Breaking up your videos into smaller 1-3 minute segments is a great idea. You can then use the same content from your YouTube video description and repeat it for each segment. This allows you to create 3-30 different video clips from a single sermon, which you can then post on all your social media platforms. There are platforms like munch.io in which you can upload your video and it will cut your videos for you. The benefit of using munch includes the programs ability

To avoid spamming your followers, it's best not to post the same video on every platform. Each social media platform has a different audience, so it's important to tailor your content to each one. By doing so, you'll be able to reach a wider audience while also catering to the unique interests and preferences of each platform's users. This strategy emphasizes the importance of knowing your audience and understanding who you're trying to reach.

Remember, creating high-quality content is key to gaining more views, likes, and shares on your church YouTube channel. Consider what your audience is interested in and tailor your content to their needs and preferences. Yes, they are following you so we hope they would be into Jesus, but what life applications can you give them? What can you help them with? What are they responding to?

There are several effective strategies for boosting your following on TikTok. Here are a few tips:

1. Post regularly: Consistency is key on TikTok. Posting frequently can help keep your content in front of your followers and increase your chances of getting discovered by new viewers.
2. Use popular hashtags: Including popular hashtags related to your content can help make your videos more discoverable to a wider audience.
3. Participate in challenges: TikTok challenges are a great way to increase your visibility and reach on the platform. Participating in popular challenges and trends can help you get noticed by other users and potentially go viral.
4. Engage with your audience: Responding to comments and messages, as well as creating content based on viewer suggestions, can help build a loyal following and increase engagement on your videos.
5. Collaborate with other creators: Collaborating with other creators can help you tap into their audience and potentially gain new followers. Look for creators who have a similar target audience or niche to yours and explore collaboration opportunities.

6. Make visually appealing content: TikTok is a highly visual platform, so creating visually appealing and creative content can help your videos stand out and potentially go viral.

Remember that growing a following on TikTok takes time and effort. It's important to stay consistent and patient while experimenting with different strategies to find what works best for your unique brand and content.

Bonus Content:

Sample Marketing Plan

Target Audience:

Our target audience is families with children between the ages of 5 and 12 who live in the surrounding neighborhoods. We also want to reach out to young adults who are seeking a faith community.

Marketing Channels:

1. Social Media - We will use Facebook and Instagram to post information about our church and upcoming events. We will also use Facebook

ads to target families in the surrounding neighborhoods.

2. Community Events - We will participate in community events such as farmers markets, festivals, and parades to promote our church and invite people to visit us.

3. Direct Mail - We will send postcards to families in the surrounding neighborhoods to invite them to our events and services.

4. Church Signage - We will place signs outside the church building to promote upcoming events and services.

Budget:

Our total marketing budget for the year is $10,000.

- Social Media Ads: $3,000
- Community Events: $2,000
- Direct Mail: $2,000
- Church Signage: $1,000
- Website Design and Maintenance: $2,000

Goals:

- Increase attendance at our Sunday services by 20%

- Increase the number of families with children who attend our church by 25%
- Increase engagement on our social media channels by 30%
- Increase donations by 15%

Measurement and Evaluation:

We will use various methods to evaluate the effectiveness of our marketing efforts, such as tracking attendance at services and events, monitoring engagement on social media channels, and tracking donations. We will also use surveys and feedback forms to gather feedback from our members and visitors to help us improve our marketing strategies.

By using these marketing channels and tracking our goals, we aim to build a stronger presence in the community and attract more members to our church.

Tips For Developing Brand Strategy

Developing a brand strategy is an important aspect of building a strong and recognizable church identity. Here are some tips and guidance on how churches can develop their own brand strategy:

1. Define Your Mission Statement and Values

A strong brand reflects the values and mission of the church. Begin by defining your church's mission statement and values. This will help you to understand what your church stands for, and what you want to communicate to your members and the wider community.

2. Identify Your Target Audience

Identify the target audience you want to reach with your brand. Who are the people you want to attract to your church? What are their interests and needs? By understanding your target audience, you can create a brand that resonates with them and speaks to their values.

3. Develop a Visual Identity

Developing a visual identity is an important part of creating a brand strategy. This includes choosing a color scheme, typography, and a logo that reflects your church's values and mission. Your visual identity should be consistent across all your church's communication channels, including your website, social media, and print materials.

4. Create Brand Guidelines

Creating brand guidelines is essential to ensure consistency in your brand messaging and visuals. This document should outline how your church's brand should be represented, including guidelines for using your logo, colors, and typography.

5. Use Your Brand in All Your Communications

Make sure to use your brand consistently in all your communications, including your website, social media, print materials, and signage. This will help to build brand recognition and reinforce your church's values and mission to your members and the wider community.

6. Monitor Your Brand's Reputation

Monitor your church's brand reputation by listening to feedback from your members and the wider community. Use feedback to make improvements to your brand strategy and to ensure that your church's brand remains relevant and reflective of its values.

By following these tips and guidance, churches can develop a strong brand strategy that reflects their values and mission, and resonates with their target audience. A strong brand can help to attract new members, build a sense of community, and communicate the church's mission to the wider community.

Rebranding

Conduct a Brand Audit

1. Before you begin redeveloping your brand, it's important to conduct a brand audit. This will help you to understand your current brand identity, including your strengths and weaknesses. A brand audit can include analyzing your website, social media channels, print materials, and other marketing collateral.

Define Your Target Audience

2. As you redevelop your brand, it's important to define your target audience. Who are the people you want to attract to your brand? What are their needs and interests? Understanding your target audience will help you to create a brand identity that resonates with them.

Refine Your Mission and Values

3. Refine your mission statement and values to ensure they align with your target audience's needs and interests. This will help you to create a brand identity that is relevant and meaningful to your target audience.

Develop a New Visual Identity

4. Develop a new visual identity that reflects your refined mission and values. This can include creating a new logo, color palette, typography, and imagery that reflects your brand's personality.

Create Brand Guidelines

5. Create brand guidelines that outline how your new brand identity should be represented across all channels. This will ensure consistency and help to build brand recognition.

Communicate Your New Brand

6. Communicate your new brand identity to your audience through a variety of channels, including your website, social media, email marketing, and print materials. This will help to build awareness and encourage engagement with your new brand.

Monitor and Adjust

7. Monitor your brand identity and adjust as needed. Collect feedback from your target audience to understand how your new brand identity is

resonating with them. Make adjustments as needed to ensure your brand is aligned with your target audience's needs and interests.

By following these tips, you can redevelop your brand identity and create a brand that is relevant, meaningful, and resonates with your target audience.

Marketing as we know it today did not exist in biblical times, but there are instances in the Bible where communication and persuasive techniques were used to promote a message or a cause. Here are some examples:

1. In the New Testament, Jesus used parables to convey his message to the masses. He used storytelling to illustrate important lessons and teachings to his followers. This was a form of persuasive communication that aimed to make his teachings more relatable and understandable.

2. In the Old Testament, the prophets used different techniques to communicate their messages to the people. For example, Jeremiah used a yoke and bonds to symbolize the coming Babylonian captivity and urged the people to submit to the king of Babylon. This was a way of making his message more tangible and relatable to the people.

3. The Book of Proverbs is full of examples of persuasive communication. The book contains various sayings and proverbs that were designed to make people think and act in a certain way. For example, Proverbs 16:24 says, "Kind words are like honey--sweet to the soul and healthy for the body." This proverb was designed to encourage people to be kind to one another and to use words that build up rather than tear down.

4. In the New Testament, the apostle Paul used persuasive communication to spread the message of Christianity. He wrote letters to the churches he founded, and these letters were designed to persuade and encourage the believers in those communities. For example, in his letter to the Romans, Paul wrote, "I am not ashamed of the gospel, because it is the power of God that brings salvation to everyone who believes" (Romans 1:16). This was a way of persuading the Roman believers to remain strong in their faith despite persecution and challenges.

Overall, the Bible contains numerous examples of persuasive communication and storytelling, which are important elements of marketing. However, it is important to note that the goal of marketing is usually to sell a product or service, whereas the messages conveyed in the Bible were often intended to promote moral and spiritual values. The focus should not be on becoming the top salesperson, but rather on comprehending the methods for effectively communicating a message. It's commonly understood that one should avoid turning their church into a dull sales pitch, as people can sense this. Instead, the goal is to comprehend one's position, identify the audience, and communicate the message efficiently.

GRANTS

There are many grants available for nonprofit organizations to fund marketing and outreach efforts. Some examples include:

1. Google Ad Grants: Nonprofits can apply for up to $10,000 per month in Google AdWords advertising credit to help drive online traffic and donations.
2. Facebook Ads for Nonprofits: Facebook offers free advertising credits to eligible nonprofit organizations to help them reach their target audiences.
3. The Newman's Own Foundation: This foundation provides grants to nonprofit organizations that

focus on nutrition, education, and/or empowering people with disabilities.

4. The Bill & Melinda Gates Foundation: This foundation provides grants for organizations working in global health, education, and poverty reduction.

5. The Coca-Cola Foundation: This foundation provides grants to nonprofit organizations working on environmental sustainability, community well-being, and education.

6. The Verizon Foundation: This foundation provides grants to nonprofit organizations working on education, domestic violence prevention, and internet safety.

7. Lilly Endowment National Clergy Renewal Program: This program offers grants of up to $50,000 to pastors and other religious leaders for sabbatical programs that can help improve their overall well-being and effectiveness.

8. Catholic Extension: This organization provides grants to Catholic churches in the United States to help them with capital projects, ministry support, and leadership development.

9. The Arthur Vining Davis Foundations: These foundations provide grants to religious organizations and theological schools that focus on religious education, leadership development, and interfaith relations.

10. The Templeton Religion Trust: This trust provides grants to organizations and individuals that explore the intersection of religion and science, as well as other topics related to spirituality and faith.

11. The United Thank Offering: This organization provides grants to Episcopal churches for projects that focus on mission and ministry. Projects can include things like outreach programs, community development initiatives, and educational resources.

12. The United Methodist Communications Grants: These grants are provided to United Methodist churches in the United States to help them with communication strategies and technology.

13. The Thriving Congregations Grant Program: This program is offered by the Lilly Endowment and provides grants to help churches in the United States enhance their ministries and outreach programs.

14. The United Church of Christ Grants: The United Church of Christ offers a variety of grants to its member churches and other organizations, including funding for new church development, environmental justice initiatives, and racial justice programs.

15. The Episcopal Evangelism Grants Program: This program provides grants to Episcopal churches in

the United States to help them develop and implement evangelism programs.

16. The Presbyterian Mission Agency Grants: This agency provides a wide range of grants to Presbyterian churches and organizations in the United States and around the world, including funding for mission work, social justice programs, and leadership development.

17. The Baptist Community Ministries: This organization provides grants to Baptist churches and other nonprofits in the Greater New Orleans area to help them with community development and health initiatives.

18. The Baptist Foundation of Alabama: This foundation provides grants to Baptist churches in Alabama to help them with capital projects, leadership development, and ministry support.

19. The Baptist Health Foundation of San Antonio: This foundation provides grants to Baptist churches and other nonprofits in the San Antonio area to support health-related initiatives and services.

20. The Cooperative Baptist Fellowship Grants: The Cooperative Baptist Fellowship provides a variety of grants to its member churches and other organizations, including funding for mission work, pastoral training, and church planting.

21. The Baptist Healing Trust: This organization provides grants to Baptist churches and other nonprofits in Middle Tennessee to support health and wellness initiatives.
22. The Community Foundation of Greater Memphis: This organization provides grants to nonprofits in the Memphis area, including churches and religious organizations like COGIC, to support a range of community initiatives.
23. The J. E. and L. E. Mabee Foundation: COGIC may be eligible to apply for grants from this foundation, which focuses on supporting Christian organizations and programs in the southwestern United States.
24. The Gulf Coast Community Foundation: This organization provides grants to nonprofits in the Gulf Coast region, including churches and religious organizations, to support education, health, and human services initiatives.
25. The African American Church Grants Program: This program is offered by the United Church of Christ and provides grants to African American churches and ministries to support a variety of initiatives, including leadership development, youth programs, and community outreach.

These are just a few examples of the many grants available for nonprofit organizations. It's important to research and apply for grants that align with your organization's mission and goals. CauseIQ has a list of donors and foundations.

https://www.causeiq.com/directory/grants/grants-for-christian-organizations/

Remember, grant availability and eligibility criteria can vary widely depending on the organization offering the grant and the specific needs of your church or ministry. It's always a good idea to do thorough research and speak with representatives of the granting organization to determine the best grant opportunities for your specific situation.

Authors Bio

Anthony Caraway is a multifaceted professional with a passion for marketing and church administration. He earned his Bachelor of Science degree in Integrative Studies with concentrations in Business Management, English, and Journalism from the University of North Texas Denton. With over a decade of experience in marketing for both nonprofit and for-profit organizations, Anthony has honed his skills in digital marketing, social media, content creation, and more.

As a Reverend, Anthony has also worked in administration, assisting several churches and denominations in building thriving communities. His experience and knowledge in marketing have allowed him to approach church administration with a unique perspective, utilizing marketing strategies to increase engagement and attract new members.

In addition to his work in marketing and church administration, Anthony is also a published author, speaker, and mentor. He is passionate about helping others achieve their goals and find success in their personal and professional lives.

Anthony's diverse background and expertise make him a valuable asset to any organization or community. Whether he is leading a marketing campaign, developing a new church program, or mentoring a young professional, Anthony is dedicated to making a positive impact in the world.

Glossary:

80/20 Rule (Pareto Principle): A concept that suggests that 80% of the results come from 20% of the efforts given to social media use. This means that 80% of engagement, reach, and interactions with an audience come from 20% of social media content.

Approach: The manner in which an organization or individual conducts their marketing efforts, which can range from passive to aggressive.

Brand Identity: The fundamental and unique set of features, messaging, and visual identity that defines an organization and sets it apart from competitors.

Branding: the process of creating a unique name, design, and image for a product or organization in the consumer's mind

Church Engagement: The act of actively involving members and visitors of the church in events, activities, and services to build a sense of community and connection.

Church outreach: The act of using social media effectively to attract new visitors to the church.

Community: a group of people with shared characteristics or interests living in the same place or having a particular characteristic in common

Consistency: The act of maintaining uniformity in branding, communication, and marketing efforts across all departments and stakeholders.

Core values: fundamental beliefs or guiding principles that define an organization's culture and behavior

Copywriting: The act of writing copy or text for the purpose of advertising or other types of marketing communications.

Data Analysis: The process of examining data in order to extract useful information and insights.

Email marketing: The practice of sending commercial messages to a group of people via email.

Email list: A group of people who have signed up to receive email messages from the church, which can be built by asking people to sign up on the website or in-person events.

Email marketing success: The measurement of email marketing campaigns' success, tracked through metrics such as open rates, click-through rates, and conversion rates.

Email regulations: Email regulations that require including an unsubscribe link in the emails and honoring unsubscribe requests promptly.

Engaging email content: The content of an email that is visually appealing, easy to read, and provides value to the reader. It includes calls-to-action that encourage the reader to take action.

Graphic Design: The art and practice of creating visual content to communicate a message to a target audience.

Hashtags: Keywords or phrases preceded by the # symbol, used on social media to help content get discovered by new members.

Inclusivity: the practice or policy of providing equal access to opportunities and resources for people who might otherwise be excluded or marginalized

Inspiring content: Sharing inspiring and uplifting content on social media that appeals to people's values and interests, such as quotes, Bible verses, and stories of people positively impacted by the church.

Introspection: the examination of one's own thoughts and feelings

Live streaming: Broadcasting events or services in real-time on social media to give members who can't attend in person the opportunity to participate.

Low-cost: inexpensive or affordable compared to other options in the same category. The specific threshold for what is considered low cost can vary depending on the context and the individual's perspective.

Metrics: Measurable data used to track and analyze the success of marketing efforts.

Mission: a statement of an organization's purpose and objectives

Online resources: Offering online resources such as sermons or podcasts that are easily accessible to new visitors to get to know the church and its teachings before attending in person.

Outreach Initiatives: Programs or activities aimed at promoting and engaging with a specific group or community.

Personalized emails: Emails that include the recipient's name in the subject line and throughout the email and are segmented based on interests or behaviors to send targeted messages.

Promotional activities: activities designed to advertise or promote a product or organization to potential customers or members

Promoting events: Using social media to promote events that may appeal to people who are not regular church-goers, such as a free community concert or a workshop on a popular topic.

Social justice: The concept of fairness and equality in the distribution of wealth, opportunities, and privileges within a society

Social media: Online platforms that allow users to create, share or exchange information, ideas, and content.

Social media discussion: Encouraging members to engage with each other by sharing their thoughts and experiences on social media through posting questions, hosting polls, or inviting members to share their own stories.

Social media influencers: Partnering with social media influencers who have a large following in the community to promote the church to their followers and attract new visitors.

Social media management: The process of creating, scheduling, analyzing, and engaging with content posted on social media platforms.

Social media resources: Sharing resources that can help members grow in their faith, such as daily devotionals or inspirational quotes, on social media.

Targeted advertising: Using social media advertising to target people in the community who are likely to be interested in the church, based on location, interests, and other demographics.

Value proposition: A unique and compelling description of the benefits a product, service or organization offers to its customers or members.

Welcoming social media presence: Creating social media profiles that reflect the welcoming and inclusive culture of the church with engaging visuals, such as high-quality photos and videos, to showcase the church and its activities.

Willing workers: The necessary personnel needed for an effective marketing team, which can vary depending on the size, goals, resources, and expertise of the church.

www.ingramcontent.com/pod-product-compliance
Lightning Source LLC
Chambersburg PA
CBHW072150230526
45467CB00042B/1620